THE

SUCCESSFUL

INTERVIEW

THE

SUCCESSFUL

INTERVIEW

99 QUESTIONS TO

ASK AND ANSWER

(AND SOME YOU SHOULDN'T)

By

STACEY A. GORDON, MBA

This book is for informational purposes only. With regard to important decisions that can potentially have significant legal, financial, or other employment consequences, no book can take the place of individual legal or other professional advice. Law and practices may differ from state to state and locality to locality, are constantly changing, and are open to differing interpretations. Readers are advised to consult a lawyer or other professional, as appropriate to the nature of their particular situation, before acting on any of the information in this book.

ISBN 13: 978-0615776057

ISBN 10: 0615776051

Printed in the United States of America.

I live by the creed that luck is what happens when preparation meets opportunity.

This book is dedicated to the overworked, underpaid, and unemployed across America who intend to be prepared.

Contents

Acknowledgements

Anyone who knows me has had the opportunity to be on the receiving end of my direct, and to-the-point, nature. It is a result of my years of New York living and I don't apologize for it. In fact, I could name a number of people who could benefit from being a little more direct every now and then (but I digress).

All that I have accomplished would not have been possible without the support of my husband who has spent many, many evenings rocking babies (ours) and cooking dinner so that I could attend graduate school classes, go to networking events (earning the moniker of "networking queen"), give presentations, plan a conference for 1000 women in another state, start a business and write this book.

I thank my mom and Victoria Pynchon for being major supporters. Without their prodding, encouragement and belief in my ability to be great, I would probably have attempted less.

To Rosemary Sneeringer (copy editor) and Keri Knutson (cover designer), I thank you for your hours of free advice, your invaluable information and expert assistance.

Most authors thank their children and I honestly don't know why. It's not as if they help you write! As I write this, my youngest daughter is alternatively yanking my hair and putting fingers into the ports on my laptop. Without my children, I could do more, but then I would have no reason to do anything.

"Choose a job you love and you will never have to work a day in your life."

-*Confucius*

Introduction

We've all been there—sitting across from a stranger who holds the key to our dream job, our opportunity to advance or our chance at more money. Our palms are slightly sweaty, and we wonder what the interviewer is thinking as they look at us. More than likely, he is a little bored. If the position has been open for a while, he is tired of interviewing candidates. If he has just started the interview process, odds are he's tired at the mere prospect of all the interviews to come.

Your interviewer is wondering just how many of you he is going to have to speak to in order to find that one person who can do the job. Because, at the end of the day, the only question an interviewer really wants you to answer is, "Can you *do* the job?"

As harrowing as the interview process can be, you can remove some of the anxiety by reminding yourself this is a two-way street. While the interviewer is examining your credentials, your background and your willingness to work, you have the opportunity to do the same.

Have you ever taken a job, only to regret it later? How many times have you been turned down for a job after an interview, only to realize later that you dodged a bullet? Not enough candidates utilize the golden opportunity they are given to ask the questions that allow them to make an intelligent decision about whether they really want to be employed by a certain company.

Preparation is the key to success. Don't just prepare for the questions you will be asked. You need to ensure you have adequately prepared questions for you—as the interviewee— to ask. You need to determine if your potential new boss is a micromanager. You would want to discover before you start the job that four people have held this position in the last 18 months and that the department you will be working in has been losing money for the past three years.

The job market is extremely competitive and in times of high unemployment, it is even worse. Unfortunately, this usually results in candidates experiencing increased discrimination. Older workers, pregnant women, and candidates with a criminal history are among the first to be hit hard by high unemployment numbers. I would like to believe employers don't discriminate, but as a Black woman in America, I can't even begin to write that and maintain a shred of credibility. So for those who may need a little extra help and encouragement, I've included a section on questions employers are not supposed to ask, but might.

I have also included a section of questions candidates usually want to ask, but shouldn't.

With that being said, the vast majority of questions you'll see presented in this book are questions frequently asked by an interviewer who seeks to gain an understanding of your proficiency in communicating, to learn more about your personality, what your body language says about you, your likability, and your ability to back up what you put in your resume. Every time you answer one of the questions in this book, you need to ensure you find a way to answer the unspoken question: Can you do the job and will we like you while you're doing it?

"Climbing to the top demands strength, whether it is to the top of Mount Everest or to the top of your career."

-Abdul Kalam

PART I

QUESTIONS AN INTERVIEWER WILL ASK YOU

"A lot of fellows nowadays have a B.A., M.D., or Ph.D. Unfortunately, they don't have a J.O.B."

-Fats Domino

Part I: Questions an Interviewer Will Ask You

I can guarantee you will not be asked all of the questions listed in this section, so you may find yourself asking, why bother reading all of them? My purpose in listing these questions is to inform you of their existence and acquaint you with their format. The motive behind each question is something you need to understand before you can begin to formulate an answer.

It will be apparent to you that some of these questions seem similar. This is to ensure you see the questions in all of their various formats and understand the interviewer's purpose for asking one question versus a different question with similar content. Once you are well positioned to see what the interviewer wants to know, how the question is asked won't intimidate you and you'll be ready for anything.

Behavioral questions can be easily answered by utilizing the STAR Method, which forces you to identify the **S**ituation, **T**ask, **A**ction and **R**esult of the situation you are discussing.

Situation: Describe the problem
Task: Define the task you needed to accomplish
Action: Describe the specific steps you took
Result: Explain the outcome

Be as specific as possible, utilize examples, don't be afraid of a negative outcome (lost the account), and don't ramble— keep to your script.

Before moving on, you may want to begin by recalling recent work situations that showcased your teamwork, initiative, planning, customer service, goal-setting and leadership. Once you have made your list of attributes, read through all of these questions, then formulate and practice your answers to prevent being caught off-guard during the interview. So, let's get started!

1. Tell me about yourself.

We have all been on interviews where we were subjected to the dreaded, "Tell me about yourself" question. It has plagued us all and we usually leave the interview feeling we did a poor job of answering this. It isn't even a real question, which just serves to vex us even more. Just what does the interviewer want to know?

The overall purpose of the entire interview is to decide if you are the person they want to hire. Your every word, gesture, expression and even what you don't say is examined and evaluated. What the interviewer wants to know is that they didn't make a mistake in inviting you to meet with them. They want to know that their time isn't being wasted and they need to know they can trust their judgment. "Tell me about yourself" means tell me about your qualifications and how they relate to the position for which you are interviewing.

Why are you here? What brought you to the point that you are now sitting across from an interviewer asking for a job? This is your time to provide your story . . . not your sob story, your professional one!

Start with your education, and then describe your past employment that is relevant to the position, including your performance. Showcase promotions, commendations, innovative ideas that were implemented, sales volume increases, etc.

I studied biology in college because I thought I wanted to be a doctor. However, by the time I graduated college, I realized I really didn't want to spend that much time in school. I was eager to start working and always had an aptitude for numbers. I regretted not taking any business courses while attending college, but I was eventually able to begin working at an entry-level job at XYZ Company and worked diligently as a research analyst. Within my first six months, I saved the company x dollars and was promoted. After working at the company for two years, I was offered a position at a smaller company, which provided me with more responsibility. I had the opportunity to expand my skills and experience because the scope of my work was larger. Two years ago, I made the decision to begin classes to enable me to earn an MBA in business. I was able to work full-time while attending school, and though it was taxing, it was also rewarding. I successfully balanced my work and school responsibilities without short-changing my employer. I now find myself seeking a new position because I have reached the ceiling of my career path at my current company with no room for growth. Since they are a smaller company with a small management team, they recognize my contributions, but don't have the ability to promote me. I would like to work for a company where I can continue to provide value while experiencing job growth and career satisfaction.

2. What are some of your best qualities?

It's an easy question, right? You're a great singer, you're the life of the party and you have a great smile. All right, I'm being a little facetious, but interviewers have heard some really stupid answers to this question. Let's remember, this is an interview for a job, so your answers should relate to the job and be professional.

An interviewer would want to know if you are always on time, have integrity, are honest (even when no one is watching), are hardworking, willing to admit mistakes, outgoing, persuasive, organized and adaptable. As you provide your list of qualities, don't forget to give examples.

I'm known for being persuasive. People have a tendency to want to join my team or support my projects because I have the ability to bring people together for a common cause. In my position at XYZ Corporation, I was able to reestablish interdepartmental meetings, which had not occurred for many years because of previous internal politics and mistrust between leadership.

Be wary of listing qualities that may paint you as an egotistical person who has trouble working in a team or who may be difficult to manage. People want to like the people they work with. Independence can hint that you like to work alone.

Decisiveness can indicate that you are rash or don't take into account other people's opinions prior to acting. The words "assertive," "bold" and even "confident" can mean "bossy" and "unmanageable."

You also don't want to create a laundry list. No one is perfect. Just stick to two or three qualities.

3. What is your greatest strength?

I know you're thinking, "Didn't we just cover that question?" And the answer is no. This question is designed to get at what you believe is your greatest strength, your best asset, and what you bring to the table that no one else can. Answers such as "fast learner," "adaptable," "I'm the 'go-to' person" or "hard worker" would be acceptable here because they work in any situation. You might want to say "fast learner" if you're interviewing for a position that is different from your previous employment. In that case you want to provide examples of what you've learned previously, how quickly you learned it and what you did to aid your learning.

If the position is one that is very similar to a past job, you may want to focus on a specific skill that is important to the job, such as a technical skill that few people possess, your aptitude with numbers (which will save the company money) or your skill with project management (which will save the company time).

Remember, you are being asked for just one strength, so it may be different for each job interview you go on. You need to adapt your strength to the position for which you are applying. Ask yourself, "Why would the interviewer care?"

4. What is your greatest weakness?

Everyone loves to hate this question. No one wants to look weak on an interview, so most people say things like "I have a tendency to work too hard," "I'm a perfectionist" or "My expectations are too high/I'm too hard on myself." And let's not forget "Ooh, that's a tough question. Umm . . ."

It's not the time to confess all of your bad habits, so you don't want to say things like "I'm always late," "I'm not a morning person" or "I don't like to be micromanaged."

So what do you say?

Try presenting your personal weakness as a professional strength.

I focus very intently when I'm working, which can cause me to seem as though I'm disengaged from my coworkers. I've had to work very hard to remember to surface once in a while and discuss my ideas with others, because you can learn from a team environment.

Or:

I am very impatient. Once a decision has been made I like to get to work immediately and sometimes this appears to others as if I'm running over them to get the work done before they have a chance. I've started communicating my work style to my coworkers so they know to expect it, but also demonstrating my passion for my work, which shows them that my impatience stems from me wanting to see the end result, not from any ill-feelings toward my coworkers.

Or:

I have a tendency to procrastinate. Even though I know a deadline is looming, I wait until the last minute to begin working on it. What I've done to prevent the possible disaster of not meeting a deadline is give myself an earlier deadline. If I have 10 days to complete a task, I cut the time down to seven. I tell myself this is to guarantee that I can review my work prior to handing it in. I know it sounds a little silly to others, but it works for me, and many times, I'm able to turn a project in early.

5. Describe yourself in three words.

Similar to the "best qualities" question, the interviewer wants to learn how you describe yourself. You can use the answers you have prepared for that question because, more than likely, the interviewer will not ask both. If "organized" is one word to describe you, remember to provide an example of why you chose this a quality and how it benefits your employer.

6. If your coworkers could describe you, what would they say?

Here the interviewer wants to know how you believe others perceive you. Be careful of the words you choose because they may be contradictory to the point you are trying to make.

If you use words like "direct," "competitive," "hard-working" or "tough, but fair," the interviewer may hear that you're difficult to work with and your coworkers don't particularly like you.

Meanwhile "outgoing," "congenial" or "caring" give the impression you're well liked, but a pushover.

None of the words chosen are negative, but the first set of words show that others respect you, but may not like you as much. This isn't necessarily a bad thing. While the second set of words give the impression you're very likeable, but they don't say much about your management style, your productivity or your professionalism.

Depending upon the type of job you are applying for, you need to make the decision about the impression you want to make and then determine which words convey it most succinctly.

7. How do you expect to contribute to this company?

Your answer is obviously going to depend upon the position for which you are applying. However, the formula is the same. In order to answer this question you must conduct research beforehand. You need to know what challenges the company is experiencing and how you might assist. Candidates have the idea that it's easier to answer this question the higher up in the company the position is placed, but that's not so.

This is a question about your motivation and should be answered with some enthusiasm. The interviewer should see that you want to work at their company, whether you're applying as Vice President of Finance or the receptionist

As VP, Finance, I understand the department's forecast of earnings will be impacted by both internal and external forces. When these situations occur it is my responsibility to ensure we act quickly to revise earning projections, to renegotiate vendor contracts and/or restructure financing to be able to meet our obligations and mitigate any losses. I have experience with overseeing challenging financial conditions and know that the relationships I have developed over time will help me to quickly make sound decisions because other departments within the company depend upon us for accurate reports.

As Receptionist at XYZ Company, I know it is my responsibility to ensure every caller receives courteous service and prompt responses. I understand that not every person who contacts the company will be respectful, and some may be rude, but it is my job to make sure their perception of the company is enhanced by each interaction with me. My positive "can-do" attitude earned me special recognition from the CEO at my prior company and I intend to increase my effectiveness in this position.

If you relate your skills and experience to a particular challenge, which, from your research, you know the company is experiencing, the interviewer will appreciate the fact that you did your homework on this particular topic.

If you're interviewing in the sales, marketing, PR, communications or legal department, you probably should make a point to mention any challenges the company may be experiencing and ask questions about it, as it may directly impact your job should you be hired.

8. Why should we hire you for this position?

If you can't come up with three really good reasons the company should hire you, the interviewer surely isn't going to do it for you. Start by analyzing your history. What have you done? What skills have you obtained? What quantitative and measureable results have you achieved?

Make a list!

If you've never done this, you might want to put this book down and do it now. You're going to need a few hours to create a cohesive list. You may even need to make a few different lists if you're seeking positions in different industries.

If you have already created your list of your skills and the results you have achieved, think about how this relates to a specific company and consider how you could be an asset. What can you do to bring value to this company? What can you offer that will be of benefit to them? This is your chance to beat your chest and proclaim your greatness to the interviewer. This is where you get to explain why you are better than the other candidates they have in their database.

You want your interviewer to start picturing you in the role. You want them to begin thinking about where your desk will be and how soon they can order your personalized stationery.

9. Why do you want to work for our company?

This is another motivation question which requires an enthusiastic answer. This is an easier question than "How do you expect to contribute to this company?" It's a softball. If the interviewer asks this question, you should be able to hit it out of the park.

Here you have the opportunity to demonstrate your knowledge of the company and show the interviewer you did your homework. Mentioning positive news articles, work they're doing in the community or spotlights on various top executives, tell the interviewer you didn't just look at the home page of the company's website. Explain how the corporate mission and vision are in line with your personal values. Make it clear why you would rather enhance this company with your skills rather than work for a competitor. Enthusiastically declare your understanding of and desire to work within their corporate culture.

10. What do you know about our company?

It may not seem like it, but this is also a motivation question. As in the question above, the interviewer wants to know you have been following their company for years and know lots of things about it them, but at the very least, they want to know you did your homework.

Not always, but sometimes the interviewer just wants to know what you know about the company rather than having to explain to you what the company does, which gives the interviewer the opportunity to fill in blanks or correct misconceptions.

Let the interviewer know what you have learned about the company from your research, but also your general knowledge of the company. If you have been following the company for a while, you should know their product lines, their reputation in the industry and public perception of the company. Show that you are genuinely interested in the company and enthusiastic about the opportunity to work there.

If you haven't bothered to find out anything about the company, how can anyone realistically believe you really want to work there?

11. If today were your first day on the job, what would you begin doing?

Remember I told you the interviewer really just wants to know you can do the job. This is a question that asks you to tell them you can get the job done. The interviewer wants to know that they're not going to have to spend a lot of time training you, explaining industry standards or walking you through the basic tasks of the job.

If you have worked in a similar position previously, explain your processes and procedures at your previous job and detail how you expect that experience to translate to the current position.

In the event the position is unfamiliar to you, explain how you believe the duties are similar to a past position and acknowledge that you will need some training in procedures specific to this company (which all candidates will need) but that the basic gist is enough for you to begin work without hand-holding.

Give examples of the software you expect to use, the administrative process you expect to be faced with and prioritize the tasks that will need to be performed. They're looking for industry lingo and an understanding of the most important functions of the job. Demonstrate you can tackle the job from day one and you'll be ahead of the game.

12. What interests you most about this position?

In this case, the interviewer really wants to know if you're aware of the most vital function of this position and if you like it. Employees who like their jobs far outperform employees who don't. If you don't know that profitability is the number one most important function in a sales position, you will not get the job no matter what else you say in the interview.

If you're a receptionist, customer service is key. If you're a webmaster, uptime is important. As a paralegal, accuracy and deadline management are vital. Know your industry, know your job, and then make sure the interviewer knows why you love it.

13. Where do you see yourself in three/five years?

The answer to this question is not, "On the other side of this desk." However, you do want to demonstrate your desire to grow within the company. If the interviewer asks where you see yourself in three years, you definitely want to see yourself working for the same company. If they ask where you expect to see yourself in five years, you don't have to explicitly say you see yourself working for the same company, but you definitely want to be in the same industry. If the company is more creative, they may not expect the same level of commitment to them as a large financial services corporation or a legal organization would. Both have a history of more static employment and less ability (or desire) to adapt.

Regardless of company size or culture, the interviewer wants to see you have a well-thought-out plan with stages that make sense. They also want to know their investment in you will be worthwhile. They need to hear you have thought about career progression, understand how it works within their company, and have sketched out a plan that is realistic and attainable within the timeframe given.

14. What are your career goals and what steps have you taken to achieve them?

Why does the interviewer care about your career goals? For the very same reason they want to know where you expect to be in three to five years. They need to assure themselves you are a worthwhile investment, but they also want to know that *you* consider yourself a worthwhile investment.

Answering this question is easier if done in two parts. Let them know your short-term and long-term goals.

In the short-term, I'd like to continue to improve upon my analytical skills while learning more about the corporate culture. I believe this will help me to communicate better with my peers and make me a more well-rounded employee.

Long-term, I see myself in a management capacity, continuing to build upon my people skills while teaching my analytical skills to others.

If asked, be prepared to define exactly what "short-term" and "long-term" mean to you in months or years.

Letting the interviewer know about specific trade publications, online learning, conferences you attend, webinars you review and professional organizations of which you are a member shows the interviewer that you consider yourself a worthwhile investment and are not relying solely on the your employer to direct you to activities and/or pay for your training. It also demonstrates your ability to self-manage.

15. What do you like most about your current/previous job?

The interviewer wants to hear that you enjoyed your job—especially if the position is very similar to the one for which you are applying. As in the "What interests you most about this position?" question, they want to know what drew you to the job in the first place. The interviewer will obtain clues about the type of employee you are from the things you say.

This is a good opportunity to show your passion for the job, your enthusiasm for the company you work for and how expertly you can do the job. Showcase your skills, your knowledge of the intricacies of the position and industry lingo.

16. Have you ever been bored with your work?

Like the question above, the interviewer is seeking to determine the type of duties you don't like to do. They want to ensure those duties aren't the major components of the job for which you are interviewing.

I've stopped being surprised at the number of candidates who apply for a job that requires knowledge of Excel spreadsheets and when asked this question, they say that working with numbers in Excel is something that bores them.

Or they're interviewing for a legal position and they say they get bored with reading contracts.

Guess who's not getting that job?

Be smart about your answer. But start by being smart about your job search. If you know you really don't like a particular aspect of a job, don't apply in the first place. Why waste everyone's time?

If you can't be passionate about the job or at least be motivated enough to fake it though a 45-minute interview, spare us all the inconvenience and hassle of reading your resume, scheduling an interview and sitting through the meeting!

Of course, this question leads directly into the next . . .

17. Why are you leaving your current employer?

If you loved your job so much, it begs the question: why are you leaving? The interviewer wants to ensure you're not seeking a job offer as a ploy to get a raise in your current job. They also want to hear if any of the reasons you are leaving exist in their own company. If so, they know you won't stick around long.

Never speak ill of a past employer. In my capacity as a job coach and as a recruiter I've spoken to candidates who left their job because of sexual harassment, unsafe working conditions, employees who were stealing, owners who were less than honest, the list goes on and on. I was privy to this information because I was not the hiring manager, and I was able to help the candidates give a truthful explanation as to why they were leaving their company without trashing anyone.

Seeking more responsibility, more variety in the projects you're assigned, opportunity for growth, imminent layoffs (where you know your department is on the chopping block and whether this information is public)—these are all reasons to leave an employer.

18. What do you like least about your current/previous job?

Once again, be wary of what you say when answering this question. You do not want to say anything negative about your employer, and you especially do not want to say anything particularly negative about the position if it's one very similar for which you are interviewing. You will also want to be careful of saying that you outgrew the position if this is a lateral move.

You need to spin a little here and be shrewd in your answer. Analyze the job duties of this new position and take special care not to mention any specific duties of your current job that you don't like that are also part of the job duties of the new position.

Put yourself in the interviewer's shoes. If part of the job requires you to drive long distances and a candidate says the part of the job they dislike most is the fact that they're on the road all the time, would you hire them?

If the position for which you are interviewing provides greater responsibility than your current/previous job, then you can provide the smallest scope of your duties as the ones which you liked the least, because, more than likely, they are aspects which would be delegated to someone else.

Think logically, look at what the new position affords you, and the answer to this question should be quite easy to put together.

19. If you were to give your current (prior) supervisor a performance review, what would s/he need to change?

I've said this before, but it warrants saying again. Do not bash your prior employer or supervisor. Negative words, tone or body language have no place in the interview.

If your supervisor is a jerk:

She is a demanding leader who is adept at motivating her employees to give their all. If she were to change anything, she could be a little friendlier. She is very focused on the task at hand and doesn't spend a lot of time fraternizing. I have learned a lot from her and I am grateful to have had the opportunity to work with her.

If you really liked your supervisor, you can feel free to gush about them. But no one is perfect.

I might suggest he change his work style so it isn't so difficult for him to dole out reprimands when results aren't as expected. When everyone gets rewarded, regardless of performance, it de-motivates the employees who really are working diligently.

20. Give me an example of a time you went above and beyond the scope of your responsibilities. How did you determine they were outside the scope, and what, if anything, did you do about it?

Instead of "Can you do the job?" this question asks "Will you do the job?" Your answer to this question tells the interviewer if you are lazy, egotistical, a clock-watcher or a team player who takes on tasks as necessary to get the job done.

As you provide your example, your body language will betray your true feelings about the situation so be certain you have practiced your answer to this question and are comfortable with the content. Many times an interviewer may hit upon something that happened many years ago, which you are still a little annoyed about. It's your job to find any old hurts and slights, define them positively with a spin of your choosing and have answers ready in the event the situation comes up in the interview.

21. Describe a time when you were faced with an unreasonable deadline. What was the outcome?

This question is actually asking for a negative. You can't avoid speaking poorly of the chump who assigned you an unreasonable task. Or can you?

Here you need to provide an example of a time when you were faced with a deadline you personally thought was unreasonable, with the outcome being that you were able to accomplish the task anyway (because you're just that good).

The trap here is that all employers believe that if they're assigning you a task, it can't possibly be unreasonable. They've already reviewed the reports and looked at the projections and determined that the task must be accomplished.

The best way to tackle this question is to define "unreasonable." What is unreasonable to you may not be unreasonable to someone else and this is where you can once again showcase your creative problem solving and teamwork.

Define the unreasonable task within the framework the employer has already created and then show that what they required exceeded it. If your job requires you to make 25 sales calls per day but you were asked to complete 60, some might say that is unreasonable.

If a marketing project usually takes 15 business days from ramp-up to completion and your boss needs it done in 3, again, some might say that was unreasonable.

Keep in mind, unreasonable doesn't necessarily equal impossible.

22. Give me your definition of "work ethic" and describe yours.

What exactly *is* your definition of "work ethic?" Have you ever defined it? If not, now is as good a time as any and a better time than on the interview.

Similar to the "scope of responsibilities" question, the interviewer is trying to determination your motivation and your willingness to go above and beyond the ordinary to get the job done.

I would define work ethic as doing what you are tasked to do in the manner in which it is expected to be done while ensuring it is done correctly and completely, even if it takes more resources and time than expected.

There are also some adjectives that can be used when describing your individual work ethic:

- Honest
- Ethical
- Responsive
- Efficient
- Dependable
- Enthusiastic
- Positive attitude

Provide an example of a time when you demonstrated this work ethic and make it one where you didn't receive recognition for it. Because that's part of a good work ethic—doing what needs to be done even when no one's looking and you're not receiving anything other than the satisfaction that you did what you were supposed to do.

23. Do you prefer to work alone or with others? Why?

There are probably times when you prefer to work alone and times when working with others makes sense. Obviously the interviewer wants to ensure you can play in the sandbox and get along well with your coworkers. They're seeking a cultural fit. Therefore, it makes sense to know the culture prior to the interview.

Explain that some projects lend themselves to working alone while others work well when you have a team. Correcting a financial report is something best done alone. However, creating a new product is something that requires input from others. Provide examples of times from your own career where you have thrived in both environments.

24. What motivates you?

Many people think the answer to this question should be money, but know they're not supposed to discuss salary, so then they think they're expected to say something about the opportunity to advance.

I had a candidate tell me what motivated her was being heard. If she believed her opinions were at least being taken into consideration, she was happy to work hard and give her all. What she didn't like was being told she could have an opinion, but feeling as though no one ever really planned to act on what she had to say.

This question gives you, as the candidate, the opportunity to express your point of view to the interviewer. If you like to be given ownership over a project or would like the opportunity to create new procedures, this is the time to say it. In the event the interviewer knows this is an environment where you will not receive that opportunity and ultimately will not thrive, they'll be doing you a favor by choosing to eliminate you from consideration.

25. Do you consider yourself to be a competitive person? How do you deal with competition?

Sales positions will usually ask something about competition. They're seeking to hire the most ambitious and cutthroat (but ethical) people they can find. If you're seeking a sales job, you're going to need to find your competitive spirit and kick it up a notch. The meek will not inherit the position.

In my previous role at ABC Company, within the first few months it was apparent that I would finish in the top five in my region. Ultimately, I earned the number two spot of 500 sales reps. Although my supervisor was ecstatic, I was already planning what I would need to do differently the next year so I would be number one!

Not seeking a sales job? Then try this:

Competition is needed to keep the job interesting. Even if I don't have a direct competitor in a coworker, I do believe you have to always strive to outdo yourself so that each time you perform, you're excelling. If we aren't getting better every day then we're stagnant, Although my position doesn't directly affect the company's standing in the industry, I believe that as a company, if each and every one of us aren't striving to continually achieve more and do more, then the company as a whole can never outdistance its competitors.

26. Besides money, how would you define job satisfaction?

Statistics show that money is not the number one thing required for job satisfaction.

Here are a few other reasons that can and should be discussed in an interview:

- The job fits my talents and interests.

- The workplace environment and corporate culture align with my personality.
- I have access to on-the-job training, coaching and mentoring.
- Diversity within the workplace is valued.
- There is opportunity for growth.
- My supervisor provides me with feedback.
- Management adequately staffs our department to assure an appropriate division of responsibilities, reducing burnout and stress levels.

For each individual, the answer will be different, and I believe you truly should be honest in answering this question if you're seeking a long-term career with this company. If you're just looking for a job "for the time being," then feel free to mold your answer into one you believe they want to hear based upon the company culture.

27. What are your greatest accomplishments?

The opportunity to brag comes along so few times in life, but no one likes an egomaniac. When answering this question, you need to find the right mix of confidence and swagger without appearing full of yourself.

This is one of those times when it's okay to use examples from your personal rather than professional life. However, I don't actually believe this. See *Part IV: Questions an Interviewer Should Not Ask You* to find out why. If you have hiked Mt. Kilimanjaro, completed a triathlon or won an award for being the best Boy Scout Troup Leader in the Western Region, you may be tempted to use this as an example.

Don't do it! Using a personal example signals the interviewer that you have nothing of note to contribute professionally and gives them information about your personal life that you don't necessarily want divulged in an interview.

So, what's an Administrative Assistant to do?

Think back to the "Why should we hire you for this position" question and dig out the list you completed. If you didn't do it then, do it now. If you're really having trouble, give experience and education as an answer while emphasizing your accomplishments.

I graduated Summa Cum Laude.

I completed a Bachelor's degree while working full-time.

I was promoted from receptionist to office manager within six months because the owner of the company recognized my work ethic and ability to learn tasks quickly.

I completed my MBA program at one of the top universities in one and a half years rather than two.

Where I believe you can utilize a personal example is in what I would consider non-employment related, but not totally personal situations. For example, if you volunteered as a fundraiser and obtained $45,000 in donations and were recognized as one of the top fundraisers, not only is this a great unselfish accomplishment, but it also demonstrates your initiative, sales skills, communications skills and the ability to be persuasive.

28. What have you learned from your mistakes?

This is another question designed to force you to divulge a negative situation. This would be the time to use an example from an early point in your career. Or if you are a recent graduate, you can utilize an example from school.

I was expected to give a presentation to our Board/Department Chairs/Executive Committee and I failed to prepare adequately. I was caught off guard by questions I should have easily been able to answer and it made me look incompetent. I never wanted to feel like that again, so rather than avoid situations where I would need to present, I seek them out. I'm now a confident presenter and I always make sure I've done my research and am prepared in advance.

29. Describe a situation where your results did not meet your supervisor's expectations. What was the outcome? What action, if any, did you take?

This question, along with the next three, is designed by an interviewer to get at the heart of the type of person you are.

Can you admit you make mistakes and can you fix them? Do you hide mistakes, blame others, or make excuses? Or do you own up, take responsibility, and look for a way to resolve the situation as quickly as possible?

When working as a recruiter for a wealth management company, I was tasked with increasing our hiring among women. Traditionally, this industry isn't one that women gravitate toward, so I worked with our marketing department to create an event that would attract women. Unfortunately, our efforts produced a smaller-than-expected attendance and we did not recruit any women at all. I was extremely disappointed in the results and my supervisor was less-than-pleased that we had, in effect, wasted the money in our budget. I decided that we needed to try again. This time I spent more time planning for the event. I reviewed the feedback from the participants at the first event, attended competitor's recruiting events and spent more time analyzing the marketing reports to understand what women were seeking in a career. Our second event was far more fruitful and we recruited 10 applicants from it—three more than required.

30. What type of work environment do you thrive in?

Have you ever really thought about this? Do you know if you prefer to work in a small, mid-size or large company, do you work well in teams, or thrive when left to your own devices?

Every company has their own unique culture, but even within departments there are variances in environments. Marketing is known for having a more creative, casual and sometimes noisy environment. The legal department or the "executive floor" is usually a quiet place with buttoned-up suits walking around and speaking in hushed tones. Smaller companies have a more congenial and somewhat family-oriented environment.

Answer the question honestly, but keep in mind, if you thrive in a quiet environment and you have applied to work in a noisy frat house type of culture, will the interviewer recommend hiring you? The ultimate question is, do you really want to work there?

31. Describe a time when you had to deal with an angry or hostile customer. How did you handle it?

The interviewer wants to be assured that if they hire you, you have the ability to represent the company calmly, professionally, swiftly and to the satisfaction of the customer— regardless of what it is the customer wants.

There are many reasons for a customer to be hostile. The customer may have made a mistake but is blaming the company anyway. You actually may have made a mistake or they could be getting the best service offered, but they just have a bad attitude. We've all met our fair share of *those* people!

In each situation, the interviewer wants to see your people skills. Explain the situation that occurred, the problem you needed to resolve, what action you took and what the outcome was. The outcome doesn't necessarily have to be positive, but the action you took should show your ability to listen patiently, clarify their problem, offer a tangible solution and not become hostile as a reaction to the customer's anger.

Ultimately, be able to show you didn't take the situation personally and your main goal was to help the customer.

32. When was the last time you lost your temper?

The interviewer is still trying to find out who you are as a person and you have now stumbled into a dilemma. You really don't want to use a professional example, because who wants to admit they've lost their temper at work? It would make you look very unprofessional. However, using a personal example is a cop-out.

For this question you will need to turn it around a little. You're not going to answer the question exactly as asked. You don't want to say that you never lose your temper because you won't be believed, but what you can admit is that there are times when you have been angry about a situation at work. Losing your temper signifies you have had some type of blow-out argument or lost your cool, both of which are unacceptable in the workplace.

During a discussion in one of our department meetings, a coworker took credit for an idea I had put forth and she was designated as our project lead because of it. At the time, I didn't see how I could say something and not be viewed as petty, so although I was very angry, I remained in the meeting without making a comment. Afterwards, I took a walk around the building to think about what happened, and, since I was still upset at the situation, I drafted an email to her, which put all of my feelings on paper. Then I made sure to delete the email. Writing it down made me feel better, and also made me realize she had taken my idea and made it better. It was difficult at first, but I put my feelings aside and worked hard on the project.

A few other reasons for losing your temper include people who are late to appointments, those who blame others for their mistakes and coworkers who consistently don't do their job, leaving you to pick up the slack.

33. Where does your current employer think you are right now?

Ooh, good question! The interview is seeking to find your level of integrity—do you have any?

If you say you told your employer you're at a doctor's appointment or that you called in sick, you admit you're a liar. So what's a liar to do?

Tell the interviewer you are using your vacation days. You want to assure them you are giving adequate time to this new opportunity and didn't want to show up rushed and watching the clock. However, be careful what you say to the person who schedules the interview over the phone; you don't want to provide contradictory information.

34. What is the most creative thing you've ever done?

If you're not interviewing for a marketing or artistic job, referring to a time when you were able to cut costs, save time and/or increase profitability will always bring a smile to the interviewer's face.

Think back over your career, your time at school and the organizations for which you may have volunteered. Ask yourself: did I produce results for a volunteer organization whose funding had been cut? Did I manage an event on a tight budget? Did I eliminate an unnecessary process and save hundreds of man-hours? Did I cut costs without reducing quality?

If you're still having problems, think of a time you came up with a creative solution to a problem.

35. Are you applying for other jobs?

You may want to dazzle the interviewer and show your desirability by naming all of the top Fortune 500 companies interested in you, but what you want to emphasize is the notion that your job search has focus. Your job search strategy should indicate you aren't just applying for every job you're remotely qualified for, but have identified companies similar to the one with which you are currently interviewing.

Don't appear scattered and desperate by naming companies in different industries with vastly different job titles. You do not want to give the impression you are just testing the waters to see what's out there. You need to present a cohesive viewpoint, which shows you are serious about the industry and type of job currently presented.

36. Describe a decision you made that was unpopular. How did you handle the situation?

It is not only managers who have the opportunity to make a decision that might annoy more than a few people on the job.

Even as an administrative assistant or entry-level clerk, the things you do affect others.

Ever changed the coffee in the break room only to hear complaints for a week? Admitted to your supervisor the overtime was no longer needed because the project had been completed early? Determined a microwave is a fire hazard and had it removed after a co-worker burned popcorn in it? Decided that food services could no longer serve cookies and cakes during meetings because they are unhealthy?

With this question, the interviewer is once again fishing to find out what type of person you are. When you made the decision did you know it was unpopular, but did it anyway? Did you gain consensus or even ask for opinions before you made the decision? Did you have the fortitude to make an unpopular decision that others were too cowardly to handle? Do you disregard the feelings of others? Are you a people- pleaser? Do you have what it takes to do what is best for the good for the company?

37. Give me an example of a problem you faced on the job. How did you resolve it?

I have had candidates tell me they had a coworker who smelled awful and no one wanted to tell her, so they stuck air fresheners under her desk. I have also had candidates who experienced sexual harassment on their jobs and attempted to resolve it, to no avail.

Honestly, these probably aren't the examples you want to go with because they're a little intense. You will want to refrain from situations that place you in a bad light, or give the impression you acted cowardly or were a bully.

Finding it difficult to leave the office on time due to workload and office culture is common. If the culture of your office is to come in late, but work late, that could cause a problem for you if you are an early riser and are usually in the office by 7:30 am.

A variation of that is when your boss simply expects everyone to be in the office as long as she is there—but she never leaves before 7:00 pm. Just us frustrating is the group of employees who leave at 6:00 pm to get dinner and then come back to work at 7:30 pm. The candidate who comes in earlier than they do has no idea of the status of the project and has to wait until late in the day to be updated.

Examples of ways candidates have resolved these "timing" issues include creating a project update log so that others can begin where someone has stopped for the day, changing the time of the staff/project meeting from the afternoon to earlier in the day, and working from home one or two evenings a week in order to be available to their coworkers who remain in the office late into the evening.

38. Share an example of how you have been able to motivate coworkers/employees.

This question asks you if you're a leader without being so bold about it. The interviewer wants to know how you inspire others, how you get them to follow you, and why others would be interested in what you have to say.

We all have leadership abilities, some of ours are a little more hidden than others. If you're seeking a management position, it would be wise to have an instance that shows you can lead by example.

Think back to a time when you helped others accomplish a goal. Leadership isn't just about what you have done, but it's about how you have pushed others forward.

Ask yourself:

- How have I helped a team to reach or even exceed its target?
- Have I helped others to adapt to a new situation?
- Have I saved a project others thought was doomed to failure?

39. What was your department's most recent success? Tell me your role in it.

Tempering the "I" in success while bragging about your achievements is a challenging task when interviewing. You don't want every sentence to begin with "I," but you need the interviewer to know how good you are. In fact, by the end of the interview, you want them to believe, as you do, that you are better than the other candidates they have interviewed, and, thus, the best person for the job.

Did your department just land a new client and you did the sales pitch? Did you make the introduction?

Your department exceeded its sales goals because you doubled your personal goals, which put everyone over the top?

Maybe a new product innovation was the result of a small tweak you suggested.

Even the legal department has its own successes. Maybe you caught a major error in a contract, which saved the company thousands of dollars in royalty fees. You successfully stopped cybersquatters from using an illegal domain name, which reduced the amount of items being sold illegally, thereby increasing profits from the authentic item being sold.

Whatever the success, ensure your role is highlighted while giving praise to the team as a whole.

40. What is your biggest pet peeve?

Similar to the question about losing your temper, this is a milder version. In that question, I advised you to tone it down, so, in this question, the answer would be the same. People who are late to appointments, those who blame others for mistakes and coworkers who consistently don't do their job, leaving you to pick up the slack are all acceptable here.

You want to show you're human without being the person in the department who is always complaining. You've worked with that person previously . . . you know, the woman in marketing who never stopped complaining about the food in the company cafeteria. Or maybe you worked with the person who always complained about the I.T. department. His questions could never be answered quickly enough, his computer never worked to his liking and it was the biggest reason he couldn't get his reports done on time.

The interviewer is trying to find out if you're *that* person so they can make sure they don't hire you.

41. What would you do if you noticed a coworker stealing?

Watch out, you're about to step into a minefield!

If you say you would do nothing, you are telling the interviewer you have no integrity and you can't be trusted (by management). If you say you would tell your supervisor about it, you're telling the interviewer you're a rat and can't be trusted (by your coworkers).

You may be tempted to say, "It depends upon what they're stealing" and all of a sudden, you're knee deep in a quagmire of your own making. Your future employer doesn't want you making decisions about what types of theft are acceptable in the office. From copy paper to petty cash, it's all theft.

You might say you would leave an anonymous note, or you could say you would tell your supervisor you noticed the petty cash drawer was short xx dollars and you suspect someone may be taking money they shouldn't. In either case, you're not identifying a specific person and it prevents you from causing major office turmoil while keeping your conscience clear.

In addition to being a trustworthy person with integrity, it lets them know you can creatively solve a problem and handle difficult situations. Which leads us to our next question . . .

42. How do you handle difficult conversations?

This question doesn't ask for a specific situation, but you're going to need to provide one in order to answer it. You could think back to a time you had to fire an employee (which will preempt the question about firing someone), a time when you had to inform a coworker they weren't pulling their weight in a team, or explain to a client you screwed up their order/project.

Maybe you replaced someone on a project who was good friends with the project leader and now he really dislikes you . . . awkward!

Give an example of the situation, the conversation you needed to have, how you prepared in advance to broach the subject and what the end result was.

I was part of a team where one of the team members was not doing their part. Everyone else on the team grumbled about it under their breath and discussed it out of earshot at the water cooler, but no one would say anything about it. After I found myself staying late each night to handle extra work for the second week, I had had enough. I took the person to lunch one day and let them know that I needed their assistance with the project. In framing it as needing help rather than berating them for doing a poor job, she realized she could be doing more on the project and began to pick up some of the slack.

43. What types of decisions do you have difficulty making?

The interviewer wants to understand which situations make you uncomfortable. Can you be counted on to make a decision when needed? Do you flip-flop or go with the majority view? Or can you be decisive?

It is customary to have difficulty making a decision that will affect a lot of people, so what you want to convey is the idea that you devote an appropriate amount of time and thought prior to making a decision. You know that while others will need to be consulted, when it comes down to it, you can be decisive and make the decision, while owning the outcome.

44. Have you ever fired anyone? If so, how did you handle it?

If you haven't fired anyone, don't think you can skip this question. Your answer may be "no" for a number of reasons:

- You gave the employee the opportunity to correct their behavior (but they quit).
- You haven't had a position of authority which would afford you the opportunity to fire someone.
- Your management style is that of the cowardly lion and your employees know you would never fire them.

However, if you haven't had the responsibility of firing someone, an interviewer wouldn't ask this question of you if they didn't believe you were at a level to where the possibility of firing someone would be necessary.

Regardless of your history, you need to make it clear that the decision to fire someone is not made lightly. Then you need to provide a situation, either real or hypothetical, that showcases your compassion when firing someone while adhering to all company rules. What were the steps you took prior to firing the person? How did you document their actions? Over what period of time did you do this?

And don't forget to mention your discussion with, and approval from, someone in the Human Resources department.

45. Do you believe it is important for a manager to gain consensus from direct reports?

If you intend to manage others, there are a number of questions attempting to get to the heart of the type of manager you are. Are you fair, direct, easygoing, tyrannical? Do you micromanage? Are you in tune with what's going on?

This question specifically seeks to determine your decision-making style. Do you work well with others or make decisions without regard to the people it will affect?

You need to walk the tightrope of showing that you value the opinions of others, but will not make a decision based solely on consensus if you don't believe it is for the good of the company.

46. How do you handle work/life balance?

A well-rounded person makes a likeable coworker. Workaholics are not fun to be around. Plus they make everyone else look bad. Employers have finally realized that health and wellness are important. They encourage healthy eating habits, they encourage vacations and they even pay their employees to get involved in the wellness programs they've instituted.

An interviewer who asks this question is looking to see if you have a life outside of work. You can say you enjoy cooking, spending quality time with family and friends or hiking on the weekends.

Don't go overboard and be very careful you don't give out personal information the interviewer doesn't need to know. Keep the response short and simple. See *Part IV: Questions an Interviewer Should Not Ask You.*

47. What do you do in your spare time?

This question is similar to the work/life balance question but is far more casual. Answer it in the same way; keep it short and simple, avoiding the trap you can fall into by talking too much. Again, s*ee Part IV: Questions an Interviewer Should Not Ask You.*

What do you say?

Mention your love of reading, but be ready to mention books that will not raise the eyebrow of the person sitting across from you. *Fifty Shades of Grey* may have been popular, but it's hardly an appropriate interview topic. Stick to safe activities that are not labor-intensive and do not involve a lot of preparation and training.

Hiking is acceptable; climbing Mt. Kilimanjaro is not.

Taking aerobics classes are acceptable; training for a seven-day triathlon is not.

Dancing—acceptable; trying out for "So You Think You Can Dance"—NOT!

Your personal life should not encroach on your work life. The interviewer should not be left wondering how you expect to find the time to enjoy your hobby and still put in a decent day, week or month of work. Plus, don't you know you only get two weeks of vacation?!

48. What is the latest book you have read?

With this question, the interviewer may be seeking to understand if you enjoy work/life balance and are reading a fictional novel or if you're brushing up in your field and are reading a professional tome that will give you an edge over the competition.

I know which impression I'd rather give. If you're interviewing in earnest, go read a book that is relevant to your profession. It can only help and it will definitely assist you in answering this question should it arise.

49. Can you explain why you held so many jobs in such a short period of time?

This is part personality question, part skills question. Remember I said all of these questions can be summed up by asking, "Can you do the job and will we like you while you're doing it?" Well, this question asks the same thing. If you were really good at what you do, you would still be working for one of your prior employers. And if people liked you, you would have a more stable job history than this.

You have to combat this assumption with promotions. The best answer to this question is evidence that you are so great at what you do that you have been recruited away to bigger, better and higher-paying positions.

Now, if you can't say that, you've got a slight problem. But not one that isn't fixable. Honestly, this is where coaching can be helpful. You need to come up with what you believe is a good explanation for your unstable job history and then get feedback from an independent person with experience in this area. The response to this question will vary greatly depending upon your actual job history and the reasons for job-hopping.

50. You're overqualified for the position.

Employers have an idea of the perfect candidate in their head, so if you hear, "You're overqualified for the position," guess what? You're not the ideal candidate. But don't be too quick to get down on yourself. Unfortunately, no one ever fits the employer's perfect portrait of an ideal employee.

If the interviewer really thought you were too overqualified for the position, they would not have invited you to interview and waste their time. Therefore, what the interviewer really wants to know is "How long do you plan to stay with our company?" Convince them you're there for the long haul and the job is yours.

On paper, I may be overqualified based on the position requirements, but I believe the term "overqualified" is very subjective. My career is not just about titles or money, but about getting the job done and being satisfied while doing it. XYZ Company is one I have always desired to work within, and this position provides me the opportunity to learn more about the company while contributing value in a way that serves the company's needs at this time. Should the opportunity arise at some future date to contribute to the company in a different capacity, I would welcome it, but at this time, and for as long as is required, it is sufficient for me to be hired at this level, performing job duties I am comfortable and well-qualified to do.

If you want someone who can and will jump right in with little training, give their all to the position and do it with lots of enthusiasm, then I am just right for this position.

Other responses could explain how this position fits into your long-term career goals. Let the interviewer know this is a job you actually want to apply for and are not just settling for because you don't believe you have any other options.

You might also be seeking a less high-stress position. However, with this reasoning, I would be careful because you could inadvertently give the impression that you're 1) lazy—seeking to get a job with less responsibility or 2) have a medical problem—the stress was getting to you. Neither of those are positive, and if you're a Baby Boomer, it will be easier for an interviewer to make these assumptions.

I will note that sometimes, when "overqualified" is used as an objection, what the interviewer really means is they didn't realize just how old you were from your resume and now that they've seen you in person, they can't hire you because they believe you'll be a drain on the company's medical, and eventually, retirement benefits. If you believe you have been discriminated against, though it may be difficult to prove, labor and employment attorneys exist for a good reason. Consult with one.

51. You don't have enough experience.

The inverse of the "overqualified" objection. So what's a recent college graduate or career changer to do?

Again, the interviewer has an idea of the perfect candidate in her head. In most cases, they also have a written job description, which provides a list of the qualifications needed to perform the most basic functions of the position. As is true for the overqualified candidate, an interviewer would not have plucked your resume from their database unless they saw something that gave them the impression you were hirable in the position. A company doesn't want to spend a lot of time and money on training inexperienced candidates, so again, we ask: what's a recent college graduate or career changer to do?

Demonstrate your ability to learn quickly—provide examples of times when you were thrown into a new situation and provide a timeline of how quickly you were up to speed or had surpassed others who had the training/knowledge prior to you.

Establish your willingness to take on tasks outside of the scope of the current job; this is where research of the company and the position will help you. If you are applying for a position that has been split in order to expand the department, or if layoffs have occurred previously within the company, then letting the interviewer know you are hungry for experience, that you want to learn and are willing to take your lumps to get it could edge out the competition, who just want to work 9-5 and go home.

Showcase your ability to perform similar or related tasks—think of volunteer positions, internships, projects performed as an assistant where you executed tasks similar to the ones you will need to do in this position.

Explain limited experience in similar positions: internships, temporary positions or additional certifications obtained demonstrate your willingness to grasp the knowledge you need for the position. You don't sit back and wait for information to come to you; you are resourceful and do what is necessary to get the job done. Though your experience may seem limited, each was necessary to set you on the path that has brought you to this interview.

52. What prompted you to return to school at this point in your career?

The answer to this question should be identical to your answer to the following question which asks, "What about your advanced degree is applicable to the position for which you are applying?"

Why? Because you should have decided to obtain a degree (whether advanced level or not) because you had a desire to advance in your career. You advance in your career by obtaining a career that is applicable to the position for which you are applying. Seems overly simple, I know, but people hear this question and immediately get defensive. They think they're being attacked and feel the need to defend their decision, and in doing so, they go overboard with disingenuous reasons that make them sound trite or egotistical.

One of the reasons to ensure you prepare for the interview is to practice your answers to questions like these so you can give a flawless answer devoid of any negative emotions. I've said it before, but your answers to most questions should be enthusiastic and give the impression that you are interested in working specifically for the company at which you are presently interviewing.

53. What about your advanced degree is applicable to the position to which you are applying?

The interviewer wants to know if obtaining yet another degree was a calculated plan or something you did because you didn't know what else to do at the time. Did you go back to school because you couldn't get a job? Did you do it to satisfy your parents? Did getting another degree make sense in light of your career plans?

More than likely, you obtained an advanced degree in order to change industries. This is a reasonable and expected answer. If it applies to you and you did not cover this in your "tell me about yourself" question, explain away!

If an industry change isn't applicable, then the answer might be, "I needed to get to the next level in my career," or "All of the managers in my department have their degrees. It's expected."

You definitely don't want your answer to be, "I was unemployed and had to move back in with my parents. They told me I couldn't stay under their roof and be idle, and since I couldn't get a job, I enrolled in classes."

54. How do you intend to handle conflicts between work and school?

This is a genuine concern of an interviewer. If you are currently attending school while seeking employment, the company expects you to be available for overtime and special projects. If you can't avoid telling your employer you're currently enrolled in classes, you're going to need to have a realistic response that will allay the fears of your potential new employer.

You could inform the interviewer that you have already tackled the more difficult courses, that you spend the majority of your weekends studying so as not to sacrifice sleep and potentially be unavailable during the week. If you only attend classes once per week, you shouldn't encounter much opposition. However, if classes meet more frequently, let the employer know you handled the workload previously and that your job is most important to you, therefore you would be willing to reduce the school course load in the event your employer found there might be a conflict. You intend to be with the company long-term, so spending additional time to complete your degree is worth it to you.

55. How have you contributed to the bottom line of your company?

If you're seeking a sales position or one related to sales, this question will most certainly arise in some form or another. The assumption is that if you were successful previously, you'll be successful again. You need to show you understand profitability is the bottom line of every company and profitability is affected by sales.

Even if you're not seeking a sales position, profitability is also affected by cost-cutting and saving time. If you've ever done anything that decreased costs, completed a project early or decreased the time it took to perform a function of your job, you have successfully impacted the bottom line of your company.

56. What special problems were you hired to solve? What did you do? What were the results?

Even if you weren't specifically hired to solve a problem, everyone encounters problems within their job. A candidate was hired to help a business owner install and manage a new accounting system, but upon starting the job, she realized the real issue was the incompetence of the clerk who was handling the billing. They didn't need a new system, they needed a new assistant. Or she needed training. In either case, how she handled that situation is just one example that can be utilized in this situation.

With this question, it's easier to work backwards. First think back through your job history and remember an issue you resolved. Did you discover a significant accounting error? Did you implement a new process? Did you create an internal product that was eventually duplicated throughout the company? What was the outcome? Once you have the outcome, utilize it as one of the reasons you were hired.

57. Did you help to establish any new goals or objectives for your company?

Regardless of the level of the position for which you are interviewing, everyone has something to contribute to the company. If you are within a large company, there are opportunities to establish goals/objectives for your department, which, in turn, affect the company.

Did you determine that the department would need to migrate from one software system to another in order to improve efficiency and add features? Did you set a goal to increase sales or productivity over a certain period of time? How did you do this? Did you have a unique approach?

Explain why the goal/objective was needed, describe the goal/objective to be accomplished, discuss the action you took to implement it and then communicate the outcome.

58. Now that you've had a chance to learn more about us, what would you change about our company?

Your interviewer wants to know a couple of things by asking this question. First, were you paying attention? If the interviewer spent time explaining some of the issues the department has been having and some of the challenges of the position, this is your opportunity to provide some insight and showcase your problem solving ability.

They don't want you to come in and shake up the place because it is imperative that before any new employee starts making major changes, they first observe the situation to see what *is* working, in addition to noting what is wrong. Tell the interviewer that, but focus on one of two minor issues that may have come up.

In the situation where it was mentioned by an interviewer that the administrative assistants kept making mistakes with forms that needed to be completed, a candidate suggested they create a binder with copies of all of the forms, complete with instructions, highlights and "sign here" post-its. This was a good non-threatening suggestion, which showed ability to comprehend the problem and quickly come up with a cost-effective and simple solution.

59. May we check your references?

Of course, the answer to this question is "yes." But what if you had a bad "break-up" with your prior employer? Maybe you weren't fired, but no one was sad to see you leave.

In the event that a mandatory reference/background check will put your future employer in contact with a person affiliated with a prior employer who may say negative things about you, there are a few things you can do.

Now hold on, I know you're thinking, "They can't say anything derogatory about me in a reference check." That may be true, but silence speaks volumes. In conducting reference checks, I've had the contact refuse to answer. They didn't say anything bad about you, but now I know they darn sure don't have anything good to say about you.

So what should you do?

Explain yourself. Explain the circumstances and why anything that person has to say is not a true representation of who you really are. Provide them with additional character references who are not family members or friends. I've never understood why people include family members or friends as references. I never contact them because they're not credible and it's a complete waste of my time and resources. It also makes me question the judgment of the candidate.

If you had a supervisor who hated everyone, let them know that. Provide examples of how that person didn't get along with anyone and that it wasn't just you. I know I advise not to badmouth an employer, but this is a special case. And you aren't "badmouthing", you're counteracting future detrimental information that could be the difference between you getting the job or not.

60. What is your current salary?

This question will probably come up. Just because *you* are not supposed to ask about money, that doesn't prohibit the interviewer from broaching the subject.

Remember that "salary" includes your base salary, plus any bonuses, commissions, expense reimbursements, and benefits, including personal days, holidays and vacation pay (at least it does in California). If you would prefer to be more accurate, you could say, "My overall compensation is approximately . . ." And if you are anticipating an increase within the next few weeks, don't forget to include that too.

61. What salary are you expecting for this position?

I know a sales guy who says, "I expect to be compensated in direct correlation to the results I achieve." Of course, this is usually a good answer when discussing commissions.

You really don't want to state a number. Any number you state will be the highest offer you can expect to obtain and if you give a number they deem as "too high," you'll price yourself out of a job without knowing it.

Salary discussions always make people nervous, so if you've been presented to the company by a recruiter, more than likely the interviewer will not ask. However, if they do, this is the time to hide behind your recruiter and use them as a shield. You can politely decline to answer and let the interviewer know that your contact prefers that all salary discussions be initiated by, and discussed, with them.

If you're not represented by a recruiter:

I believe that my skills and experience make me the best fit for the position and I'm even more convinced of this at the near conclusion of this interview. I am confident that if you agree, you will extend an offer that is fair, while rising to meet both industry and company standards.

62. Tell me something about yourself I wouldn't know from reading your resume.

This is another wide-open opportunity to discuss your professional life, not your personal life. Remember your "greatest accomplishment?" I gave the example of someone who volunteered to raise funds for a non-profit organization, and, after raising a significant amount of money, was recognized as one of their top fundraisers. This example would work here also.

If asked this question, this is a chance to discuss additional skills, certifications, and accolades that show you are a motivated, hardworking and successful individual, even though the example may not relate directly to the job for which you are interviewing.

63. Do you have any questions for me?

Why, I'm so glad you asked . . .

PART II

QUESTIONS TO ASK AN INTERVIEWER

"The biggest mistake you can make is to believe that you are working for somebody else. Job security is gone. The driving force of a career must come from the individual. Remember: Jobs are owned by the company, you own your career!"

-Earl Nightingale

Part II: Questions to Ask an Interviewer

Interviewers really dislike it when they ask a candidate if they have any questions and the answer is no. They expect you to be curious about where you intend to work, and a lack of questions indicates a lack of interest in the company, a lack of enthusiasm about the job, and, to some extent, a lack of commitment to the interview process.

When asked whether you have any questions for the interviewer, the answer is always yes. If you had the good fortune to interview with a person who spoke non-stop about the company and answered every question you had ready to ask, ask it again anyway. Ask them to clarify, ask them if there are any additional duties they forgot to mention that they believe are important to the position.

I had a question about the duties of the position and you described them in great detail. However, could you remind me of the name of the software you use in this department?

This is your opportunity to find out as much as you can about your future employer *before* choosing to work for them. And when you have a choice of job offers, this step is crucial. You don't want to find yourself in a job you hate and realize it could have been easily avoided by obtaining the answers to a few basic questions.

64. Why did you initially choose to work for this company and how did you get started?

Asking a question about the interviewer gives them a chance to discuss their own career path and it takes them off the offensive. They may be gearing up to answer difficult questions, and, like the "Tell me about yourself" question, this provides the opportunity for the interviewer to speak without restraint.

Depending upon the department they're in, if they have worked for the company for more than a couple of years, asking this question should also give you some insight into the promotional path within the company (or lack thereof) as you hope the interviewer is not still in the same position they started in.

Why do you want to know? You want to hear if they still have enthusiasm and excitement about their job. Or have they now become a tired clock-watcher? If you hear regret in their voice rather than optimism, it's just one more piece of the puzzle for you.

65. What do you like most about working for the company?

I once asked an interviewer to tell me what she liked most about her job and she proceeded to tell me she spent the day discussing results with all of her managers and how they could do better, when she would rather be out opening up more offices and hiring new managers. This tidbit of information told me that she enjoyed being out in the field and that she wasn't a micromanager. It also told me she was not pleased with the productivity of her current managers. Good information to know.

When asking this question look at the body language of the interviewer. Are they tight-lipped, do they roll their eyes, do they sigh . . . ?

66. Describe a typical day for the person in this position.

Curiosity about the position is expected, so if the interviewer doesn't hear this question, they may wonder about your interest level. More than likely, the interviewer would have previously provided information about the position as part of the interview, so don't ask a question that has already been answered. However, a variation on this question might be: "*You mentioned the position requires someone who is decisive. Can you tell me which responsibilities require this personality trait and how it relates to the overall duties of the position*"?

Why do you want to know? You need to figure out if you can honestly do this job. You also need to figure out if this is a job you really *want* to do. Do the job duties differ from what's in the job description? Will you be happy and content doing this job every day or will you be bored and seeking new employment in six months?

67. Is this a newly-created position? If yes, have you considered internal candidates for the position? If no, what caused the last person to leave?

You need to know what happened to the person who had this position before. It's a little like being the royal taste tester. If you find out the prior taste tester died, you might have some misgivings about the job.

Did the prior person get frustrated and quit? What was frustrating her? Is your soon-to-be supervisor a micromanager who works his employees to death? Is he hated? Does he have a reputation for being inappropriate? Sure, you may not actually get the direct answer to these questions, but finding out exactly why the prior person left gives you an insight into company behaviors, expectations, results achieved (or not) and your soon-to-be supervisor's personality.

You really have to ask the question and then listen to what they say, and don't say. Pay attention and don't be in a hurry to interrupt with your own story. You want to give them as much opportunity as possible to divulge as much information as possible.

68. How long has this position been open?

The interviewer may not be extremely forthcoming with the answer to this question, but in the event that happens, you can probably assume the position has been open for quite a while.

Why do you want to know? It gives you an insight into how difficult it has been for them to fill the position. Maybe they are being quite unrealistic in their expectations and can't find anyone suitable (in their eyes). It may also hint about the importance of this position. Is it a priority or not? If they're dragging their feet on hiring someone, what's happening to the work that should be getting done in the meantime? What type of backlog will you encounter if you take this job?

69. How many people have held this job within the last 5 years?

Is there longevity within the department and within the company or are you about to step into a revolving door? If people have been quitting every six months (or worse yet, being fired), there is a problem that will probably not be resolved if you are ultimately hired. If you have a choice of jobs, this may be the one you pass up unless they can give you a really good reason why this has occurred and assure you the problem has been handled, i.e. the supervisor with the unrealistic expectations has been fired.

70. Will there be an opportunity to meet with my potential coworkers during the interview process?

Having the opportunity to speak with coworkers can really give you the inside track of what's going on. I once had a candidate whose potential coworker told her to "Watch her back" if she took the job. Needless to say, she didn't accept the offer.

Coworkers can give priceless nuggets of information. They're not bound by rules of HR and you can get a gauge of both department politics and company culture by speaking to them. Their demeanor—despondent, enthusiastic or irritable—speaks volumes!

Meeting your coworkers can also give you a sense of department culture. You may get to see their workspace and obtain a good picture of what it would be like to work there. More importantly, do you like these people? First impressions are important and wouldn't it be preferable to meet your coworkers prior to accepting the job?

71. Describe the type of person you believe would be successful in this position.

You want to know if they know what they're looking for. As a recruiter, there's nothing worse than sending candidates to interview with a company who think they know what they're looking for in a candidate only to have them turn away great candidate after great candidate. When you ask what was wrong with them, they say they didn't fit the culture or they didn't "click" with the management team. Six months later they call to inquire whether "so and so" is still available.

As a candidate, you want to know what they're looking for so you can take a hard look at your own experience and qualifications to see if you measure up. You also want to see if they're logical in what they're asking for.

Asking for someone who is good with numbers, when, to your knowledge, the position doesn't require any type of work with accounting or figures gives you the opportunity to ask follow-up questions and discover why this skill is necessary. You may find out there is more to the job than you knew.

72. What are some of the traits you have identified in employees who have had a difficult time with this position?

I encourage candidates to ask this question because the interviewer gets to tell you all the things they hated about the prior person in the job. Maybe they couldn't figure out the advanced features of Excel and their spreadsheets were always a mess. They didn't listen well and thought they had the job figured out so they weren't open to suggestions. They didn't work well in teams. They didn't accept responsibility. Their customer service skills were lacking . . . This is great information to know because you, as the person who could potentially be doing this job, get a candid look at the position and some of its difficulties.

It gives you time to review just how this job really works and weigh some of the downsides. You also get to take a long hard look at yourself and ask, "Can I do this job?"

73. What is the main result you are expecting the successful candidate to accomplish? How successful was the prior person in achieving it?

Getting to know the expectations of the position prior to accepting the job is probably a good idea. You will get the opportunity to decide if you really want to do this particular job based upon the core competencies that will be expected of you. Do you really want to produce the expected output consistently every day without fail?

Hearing someone's description of what they expect is very different from reading the job duties written on paper. Listening to the interviewer describe what is expected and then hearing how someone else either excelled or failed at it only serves to add to the picture being painted.

Has your opinion of the job changed? Is the outlook better than you first imagined? Can you picture yourself working there? If you're not excited about the main responsibilities of the job as described, this is a good indicator that this may not be the job for you.

74. What is one thing I could do that would benefit you most in this position?

Though this is a slight variation on the "main results" question above, where that question asks for a general answer, this question specifically asks the interviewer how you can help them. It's a subtle difference and you probably won't ask both questions, but depending upon the job, one may serve you better than the other.

75. Do you believe the result you expect is reasonable and attainable?

It's a bit of a gutsy question, but asking this question as a follow-up to the prior ones makes the interviewer give the rationale behind the result they're seeking. It also gives you some insight into how they make decisions.

Remember, this is your opportunity to find out if you want to work there. Do you want to find yourself in a position where the expectation is unrealistic? Are their sales goals more than double the expectation in your prior position? Is the territory larger with fewer resources to manage it?

Don't set yourself up for failure.

76. What tools/guidelines do you use to measure results?

Staying along the lines of goals and outputs, KPIs are called "key performance indicators" for a reason. They usually turn up at the end of the year when it's time for performance reviews. Asking about expected results and tools for measuring them up front, *before* you accept the job prevents you from having unexpected and incomplete goals. This gives you the opportunity to make sure you begin working toward the desired results from day one.

77. Based upon your initial assessment of my skills, how do you think I would fit into this position?

This question serves to get a good gauge of where the interviewer has placed you among the other potential candidates. She has already ranked you by this point in the interview and she is either mentally discussing the next steps in the process or wondering how soon you will stop asking questions so she can end the interview.

Her answer to this question will provide you with more clues. She may be honest and say she has some concerns about your abilities. In which case, you now have the time to discuss this in person and counter any points she has made. Or she may say she is cautiously optimistic about your candidacy and looks forward to moving you forward in the process.

You get the chance to counteract any negatives and turn them into positives or you know you're a front-runner for the position. Either way, you win.

78. Who does this position report to? (If the interviewer isn't this person.)

The obvious reason to want to know who this position reports to is to get a sense of hierarchy; not just for reasons of ego, but knowing who the position reports to and who your superior reports to gives you a sense of just how difficult it may be to get things done. How hard will it be to gain consensus, be promoted, and obtain department resources?

I had a paralegal candidate who had the choice between working for two large law firms. In the first, she would be reporting to the Senior Paralegal who reported to a Staff Attorney who reported to a Senior Associate who reported to a Junior Partner who reported to a Senior Partner. In the second firm, she would report to an attorney who reported to a partner.

Which job do you think she chose?

79. How much has the department grown in comparison to the overall growth of the company?

No, you're not expecting the interviewer to pull out graphs, charts, facts and figures. But what you want to know is how important is this department relevant to the rest of the company. Is this the black hole of the company that everyone avoids being transferred into where good things go in, but nothing comes out?

Is it well-known that the department is on the verge of layoffs and you could be out of a job in 6 months? Try to get a gauge of the division by asking how it interacts with the others. Does this department put out a report the others rely upon? Is it tied to a specific product that isn't doing well? Or is it providing information across all product lines?

80. In your opinion, what is the reputation of the company within its industry?

Prior to asking this question, you need to have done your research. You should know what the answer is prior to asking. What you want to know is whether or not the interviewer is aware of the company's reputation within the industry and if they will be honest. Will they discuss a bad reputation head-on or will they ignore the fact that they were just downgraded by Moody's, their stock has fallen $25 in the past few days and their CEO is being investigated by the SEC?

Then you want to know if they will give you a reasonable explanation for the turmoil and a company plan for rebuilding.

81. How would you describe the overall management style of the company?

Another question designed to get at the type of management you will be dealing with. If you are seeking a management level position or higher, it's imperative for you to know the company culture with regard to management decisions.

Similar to knowing about the hierarchy, you need an idea of the company landscape. Some of this should be apparent from the type of company they are, the age of the company and the industry it's in. If you're going to work at a large financial institution that has been around for 100 years, you're probably going to encounter an overall management style where changes have to be vetted by various layers of management and it takes a long while to happen. However, if you're interviewing with a marketing company that has only been around for five years, odds are, the management style will be a little less "old world."

PART III

QUESTIONS YOU SHOULD NOT ASK AN INTERVIEWER

"The best time to start thinking about retirement is before your boss does."

-Unknown

Part III: Questions You Should Not Ask an Interviewer

You don't go into an interview asking "What's in it for me?" Candidates who do this come across as desperate. Especially on a first interview, your job is to let the interviewer know what you bring to *them*. I had a candidate explain that she was late (which you will never be if you want the job) because she was sharing a car with her husband, as her car was repossessed. I'm listening to her, but I'm thinking, "Did she really just tell me that?"

FYI, the interviewer doesn't care that your car just got repossessed, your daughter's college tuition is due, your mortgage hasn't been paid in two months or that your unemployment benefits have ended. These tidbits of information will not make the interviewer feel sorry for you and therefore give you the job. In fact, divulging these facts has the opposite effect.

Asking the questions in this section tells the interviewer you don't know the first thing about how to interview for a job and it makes them inclined not to offer you one.

82. What is the salary? What benefits do you offer?

Discussing money and how much you need to the job is a sure way to be rejected. Before applying for the job, but most definitely prior to the interview, you should have a general idea of the salary range. If you don't, you are not doing adequate research, you're not doing a proper job search and you cannot ever expect to have a hope of obtaining a job you will be satisfied with anytime soon.

There are many resources you can utilize to help you in your job search. Glassdoor.com is a good one, as is Robert Half's career guide and Monster.com's salary calculator. Salary.com provides job descriptions with salary information and it takes into account the cost of living for the city in which you live.

83. How many vacation/sick days/holidays does the company provide?

Similar to the above, you are giving the interviewer the impression the main thing you care about is how many days you don't have to work. The point of the interview is to show how much you want to work (for the company). Also, most companies give the standard holidays and two weeks of vacation time. Sick day policies and additional vacation days vary from company to company and that's something you'll usually find out in your job offer packet.

When job descriptions state "great benefits" or "generous benefits," what that usually means is the company still provides some type of matching program for your 401(k) plan and they offer a plethora of additional benefits such as Long Term

Care, Legal Plans, mental health assistance—all of which probably require payroll deductions. If you're so concerned about great benefits, go work for Microsoft or Apple. Otherwise, remember that the best benefit of a job is a steady paycheck!

84. What is the next step? / How do I get promoted?

This question is tricky. You may want to know what the next rung of the career ladder holds for you if you accept this job; and career growth may be the main factor for your seeking new employment. If that's the case, there are ways to find out the answer to this question without actually asking it. As discussed earlier, you can ask if this is a newly created position or if the prior person in the position was promoted.

You may be able to determine career progression by doing more research. LinkedIn is a great tool for this. If the company is large enough, you should be able to find people with the current job title. Upon reviewing their profile, you can see if they still work for the same company, and if so, you can review their new title and duties. You can also discover some of this information through Glassdoor.com.

85. What does this company do?

This is a no-brainer. Meaning, if you ask this question, the interviewer will assume you have no brain.

Seriously, I know I keep harping on this, but do your research. Never ask a question of the interviewer that can be easily answered by an Internet search. You and Google should be really good friends by now.

86. How close are you to public transportation?

You may well enjoy the option to park and ride and you hate traffic just as much as the next person, but asking this question can give the interviewer the assumption you don't have reliable transportation. Also, it's another one of those things you can figure out on your own.

87. Why did the company experience layoffs?

All right, so you've finally done some research. You notice that layoffs occurred a few months ago and you want to know what happened. Well, before I begin congratulating you, realize that if you found the information about the layoffs, reading a little more may have provided you with the answer of why they occurred in the first place.

Here's the good news (is there ever really good news when discussing layoffs?) . . . you can ask the interviewer their opinion of how the layoffs have affected business. Just don't ask them "why" they occurred. Asking why puts the interviewer on the defensive and you want to keep the interview on a positive note. Their answer may be that they cut a product line that was losing money in order to be more competitive in the market.

Don't be surprised if the person interviewing you does not have a good answer to this question. Not everyone is all that well-informed about what their company is doing. Besides, they already have the job—they don't have to do any research!

88. Who is your competition?

Once again, this question indicates you haven't done your research and are unprepared for the interview. Worse yet, it shows a lack of knowledge of the industry as a whole.

You could ask, "Between ABC Company and XYZ Company, which do you believe is the bigger competitor?" This question shows you know some of the company's competitors, you have an understanding of the players in the industry and you value the interviewer's opinion on the subject.

89. Can I work from home?

Unless the job description states there is a possibility of working from home, don't mention it. If you know the company has employees who work from home, still don't mention it. This is another, "What's in it for me?" question which only serves to allow the interviewer to question your motivation.

90. Will I have my own office?

Of course you're curious. You don't want to sit in a cubicle. Maybe you're used to having your own office and find it difficult to concentrate in an area where others are chattering away about their dates last night or complaining about their boss. You still can't ask. It just makes you look self-centered.

It is assumed from certain positions such as secretary or clerk that you will not have an office. Other positions such as VP or even manager give the impression an office will be provided. But you don't know for sure, and you won't unless it's explicitly mentioned by the interviewer. I've known secretaries who had their own office and I've known VPs who sat in cubicles—it all depends upon the culture and size of the company.

91. Will I need to complete a background check/drug test?

Asking this question gives the impression you have something to hide. If I were an interviewer and you asked this question, if I wasn't planning to conduct a background or drug test, I'm definitely beginning to question that decision now.

Certain jobs such as those within the aerospace industry, financial services, banking and insurance will definitely require this type of review. But even within these industries, the type of position you apply for will determine how thoroughly you will need to be screened.

PART IV

QUESTIONS AN INTERVIEWER SHOULD NOT ASK YOU

"A career is wonderful, but you can't curl up
with it on a cold night."

-*Marilyn Monroe*

Part IV: Questions an Interviewer Should Not Ask You

There are many reasons interviewers ask questions they shouldn't. Most of the reasons are due to ignorance of the law, overfriendliness or just plain old curiosity. There are only 500 Fortune 500 companies, but there are more than 5 million small businesses that employ over 40 million people. Most of these businesses do not have a large HR department with employment law attorneys on speed dial. More than likely, the person interviewing you is more concerned about finding someone who can do the job quickly than they are about illegal interview questions.

In general, questions about your marital status, parental status, religion, race, age, national origin, or disabilities will be avoided. But when asked, this section will help you identify and appropriately respond to questions that may arise but shouldn't.

DON'T volunteer information the interviewer doesn't need to know and isn't allowed to ask.

Many people fall into the trap of commenting on the interviewer's photo of their happy family. You may be tempted to say they have a beautiful family and their child is about the same age as yours. Don't do it. This is a "gotcha" moment. Now they know you have children, how many and what their ages are and they didn't have to ask a single illegal question to get the information.

92. This position requires a lot of travel. Is this something you can handle with small children in the home?

If you've already made the gaff of letting the employer know you have children, this question may come up. They also may ask if you can handle long hours. In the event this happens, let the interviewer know you have created work/life balance and have put in place a number of measures to ensure your career and work life are not adversely affected by your home life. You will need to assure the interviewer (without spending too much time on the subject) your career is important to you and your family understands the concept.

Give examples, which may include having a nanny, a supportive spouse, trusted providers (friends) who can pick up your children from school in the event of an emergency, etc.

Traveling with your family takes a lot of planning and organizational skills; qualities which make you an excellent candidate for the position.

93. Do you belong to a club or social organization?

Most interviewers refrain from asking questions that may require you to reveal political or religious affiliations. You can say you are a member of a professional (trade) organization that is relevant to the industry and name the organization. However, if your resume already lists all of the organizations to which you belong, the employer can ask you about them.

Ensure the organizations listed on your resume are relevant to the job. If you are your child's soccer coach, you sing in the choir at church or you are a member of your local surfing club, don't list it. If you are a soccer coach, not only will the employer assume you have young children, but they will also see it as something that can interfere with your work schedule. If you sing in the choir, it reveals religious affiliations and there are lots of stereotypes about surfers that you can avoid by removing this superfluous tidbit of information. The same is true for vintage car restoration, motorcycle club membership, involvement in a moms club or working as a yoga instructor on the weekend. These activities have nothing to do with your ability to perform your job and only serve to create obstacles to obtaining employment.

94. How do you feel about working for a manager who is older/younger than you?

This question isn't technically on the list of questions an interviewer shouldn't ask. However, an interviewer is not allowed to ask how old you are, so a question like this, related to age, takes the interviewer down a slippery slope and should be avoided.

So how do you answer it?

The duties of the job are what are most important to me. As long as what I am asked to do is within the scope of my responsibilities, I grant everyone the same respect regardless of age, gender, or ethnicity.
Answering the question this way should remind the interviewer they are on shaky ground and they will more than likely move on to the next question.

95. Are you pregnant or do you plan to have children?

If you're pregnant and seeking a job, your absence from the job is a short-term issue and you don't intend to be a short-term employee. I have not encountered anyone who expected to take more than the customary six-week maternity leave in the event they have worked for the company for less than two years. If you know you're intending to take a longer maternity leave, you should be seeking temporary work, not a full-time position.

With that being said, gone are the days (I hope) where an employer will blatantly ask if you're pregnant or plan to have children. But if it is not yet apparent from looking at you that you're pregnant, some complicated issues arise.

Let's look at it from the employer's point of view. How would you feel if a candidate you just hired says to you, "Thanks for the job, and by the way, I'm pregnant?" I think you would feel betrayed and unprepared. Here you thought you hired someone who is going to get to work and instead, you find out that this person will be leaving you short-handed in a few short months.

As harsh as that sounds, my advice, and the consensus of other experts is: Don't tell!

The employer may feel upset and betrayed, but they would not have hired you if they knew in advance. Ask any HR person and they'll agree if they're being honest with themselves. Why would they hire you? They've had the position vacant for weeks—maybe months—and they're not about to hire someone who very shortly will be gone again. This creates a dilemma for HR because they're not supposed to take pregnancy into consideration. But what's been said cannot be unsaid. How many people can honestly say they could discount the fact that the candidate is pregnant and make a decision based solely on merit?

But here is your saving grace . . . you are not required to tell, therefore you have not done anything wrong by withholding the information and not informing the interviewer.

What *is* wrong is not coming up with a viable plan for how your work will get done while you're gone. While on the job, you will need to ensure your work gets done promptly and accurately the first time. You will need to get up to speed exceeding quickly and you will need to be seen as an asset to the organization— and you will only have a few short months to accomplish this.

Here is another reason not to tell: miscarriages affect a vast number of women. What happens to the woman who tells the interviewer she is pregnant, doesn't get the job and then has a miscarriage? She is now left to wonder if she didn't get the job on her merit or if it was because she was pregnant. As devastating as a miscarriage is, no one needs the added disappointment of a failed job interview haunting her thoughts.

Finally, pregnancy discrimination laws differ in a number of states. California has a great policy on the matter, but in many states employers with fewer than 15 employees aren't subject to the pregnancy disability laws, so if you're pregnant and interviewing, check your state labor laws beforehand.

96. Can you please explain this large gap in your employment history?

There is nothing wrong with the interviewer asking this question. In fact, we would question the authenticity of the interviewer if they didn't, but you really, really wish they couldn't ask—especially when your gap is difficult to explain.

I've added this question in this section because some of the reasons for the gap in your employment may be related to questions an employer can't ask. But let me reiterate, although an employer cannot legally ask certain questions, this does not prevent you as the candidate from disclosing. Sometimes, you don't have much of a choice.

I've interviewed men whose gap in their resume was due to a decision to be the parent who stayed home to take care of the children. When that happens, the assumption is always that he only stayed home because he couldn't find work.

A man in this situation will have to overcome the assumption that he was not employable. He will have to discuss the personal decision that was made as a family to have one parent remain in the home while their children were young. Then he will have to make the decision to put his ego aside and explain that his spouse's ability to earn more money than he could at that point in his career was the reason for their decision, not his inability to get a job in his industry.

Sabbaticals are another reason for gaps in employment. You will want to make the case that the sabbatical was more of a philanthropic adventure than a need for a mental health break. Showing that you were advanced enough in your career and earnings to be able to sustain a prolonged absence will be important.

If you were lucky enough to be in a position to be out of the work force for an extended period of time, present it that way. Discuss your choice to pursue a personal aspiration that has now been completed, to care for a sick relative, or to volunteer to help rebuild a town after a disaster.

Depending upon the length of the absence, other explanations may include volunteering in order to learn new skills as you attempted a career change. Maybe you started a consulting practice in order to take on different projects within your industry, but now you miss the buzz of an office environment.

The interviewer mainly wants to know that there isn't a non-traditional reason for the gaps in your employment. If you were in jail, on the run from the law, in a drug-induced haze, in a mental institution or in rehab, you're going to need to be truthful—to an extent.

There are many organizations that can help place you in a job if your gap in employment is due to one of the non-traditional reasons mentioned above. See *Appendix II* for a list of resources that may help.

97. Would you please log into your FaceBook page/ Provide your FaceBook password?

Some companies do not allow their employees to participate in social media or hold accounts. Financial institutions, wealth managers, government personnel and teachers most notably are not allowed to have a FaceBook or LinkedIn account. The legality of such a practice is something you will need to take up with your attorney.

However, should you be faced with an interviewer who requests access to your social media accounts, try this on for size.

It is extremely important that privacy is upheld so if I were to be employed by XYZ Company, I would guard private company information just as seriously as I guard my own. I understand why you may want to review my social media activity and you are welcome to review information made public on the Internet. I am optimistic that my declining your request would not cause me to lose the opportunity to work with you and encourage you to recognize that if I were presented with a similar request for private information owned by XYZ Company, I would respond in the same way.

98. Have you ever been arrested?

The answer to this question depends upon the state in which you live. I will start with California because that is where I live.

In California, it is illegal for an employer to ask a candidate if they have ever been arrested. This also applies to cases that were dismissed in your favor, juvenile cases and sealed convictions.

Note that asking if you have ever been charged with a crime is another way of asking if you have ever been arrested.

Since this issue can be complicated, an employer may ask this question even if it is illegal. If that happens, you should be able to answer the question with a "no" as long as the arrest did not lead to a conviction.

No rule is ever completely black-and-white; so of course, there are exceptions, which include federal jobs and law enforcement jobs. But as with all aspects of this question, you really should consult with your attorney to be sure.

If you live in any other state where asking this question is illegal, such as Hawaii, Illinois, Massachusetts, Michigan, New York, Ohio, Rhode Island, Utah and Wisconsin, then the answer would be the same for you as well.

So what do you do if you live in a state where it is not illegal to ask if you have ever been arrested during a job interview or on a job application?

Well, you have to answer truthfully, but briefly. Simply answer yes and if details are requested, list the date and the offense.

During the interview, you may be asked to explain the circumstances surrounding the arrest, and if that happens, keep it brief. If there was no conviction, explain how you came to be arrested, let them know it was a one-time, unfortunate occurrence and the fact that there was no conviction will weigh heavily in your favor.

People are arrested for many reasons—you tried to break up a fight between friends and the fight got out of hand, you were the victim of an abusive partner and had to defend yourself, you were in the wrong place at the wrong time and have learned from your mistake . . . all understandable and explainable.

If your arrest led to a conviction, keep reading . . .

99. Explain the circumstances surrounding your felony conviction.

Notice this question specifically asks about a felony conviction. Usually the question will present itself on a job application, and in California, it should read as follows:

During the last 7 years, have you been convicted of a felony? (Applicant may answer the question "no" for conviction involving referrals to or participation in any pretrial or post trial diversion or alternative programs, sealed, expunged, eradicated or erased convictions and convictions for the possession of marijuana that are more than two (2) years old (except for felony convictions for the possessions of marijuana on school grounds or possession of concentrated cannabis).)

Massachusetts, Hawaii and Pennsylvania have taken this one step further. In these three states, you are not required to answer this question and can mark "not applicable" on the application. However, criminal history information may be requested, and considered, at a later point in the hiring process, to the extent permitted by law.

"Have you been convicted of a crime in the past 7 years" is a very different question than "Have you been convicted of a felony within the past 7 years?"

The first question includes misdemeanors, the second one doesn't. There is also a time limit on both. Read the question carefully! Don't answer questions that weren't asked.

The counterpoint to that is _do_ answer questions that are asked. As a general rule, honesty is the best policy and if a legal question is specifically asked, ensure you answer it honestly. If they find out you lied during the interview process, they will now assume you have a problem with honesty as well as with the law, and the odds of you being hired will dwindle dramatically. If you are hired by the company without them discovering you lied on the job application and they find out about it later, you can (and probably will) be fired.

Once you have figured out you do need to answer the question, then list the arrest date, the disposition date, what you were convicted of and the sentence. Though the application may ask you to "explain," providing the statute or code of your conviction should be sufficient rather writing out the name of the conviction. They're going to ask about it on the interview anyway.

Which brings us to the interview. Briefly explain the circumstances surrounding the arrest and spend most of your time demonstrating your rehabilitation. Highlight your successes and accomplishments since the incident and provide evidence of your rehabilitation. You may have treatment letters, letters from your clergy or a recommendation from a counselor that you can present.

Of course, you really should consult with your attorney to ensure you are armed with all of the resources you need to navigate the intricacies of getting a job post-conviction.

APPENDIX:

INTERVIEW PREPARATION AND JOB SEARCH RESOURCES

"Luckiest are the prepared."

-*Unknown*

Appendix I: Resources for Interview Preparation

Throughout this guide, it should have become readily apparent that you need to conduct research in order to be appropriately prepared for your interview. You need to know what the company does, its current financial condition, competitor information, product knowledge, industry standings, etc.

To help with your research, I have provided a list of websites to aid you in your preparation.

Salary Research / Company Reviews / Competitor Info

www.salary.com
Salary calculations are provided by searching for a job to see how much it pays.

www.glassdoor.com
A free inside look at jobs and companies including salary details, company reviews and questions interviewers have asked.

www.sec.gov/edgar/searchedgar/webusers.htm
This online database includes company reports which contain financial data and company plans.

www.vault.com
Join for free to obtain job listings, employer rankings, and
company and industry overviews. A paid membership is
required to obtain salary and employer research reports.

Driving Directions / Area Maps

Never be late to an interview again. Ensure you have mapped
your route and even practiced the route in advance with the
use of one (or more) of these websites.

http://maps.google.com

http://maps.yahoo.com

If you don't have time to drive the route beforehand, but
would like to scope out the area, know what the building looks
like and get a general idea of the area where the company is
located, check out Google Earth. http://earth.google.com

General Internet Search

Google is your friend! I don't have stock in Google so I don't
particularly care which search engine you use, but going on an
interview without doing the most cursory of Internet searches
is like going for a bike ride without wheels. It just doesn't
work.

If you are intending to work at a company, you should be
curious about recent news, old news, industry reputation,

employee comments, law suits, product recalls, impending layoffs, scandals involving embezzlement, sexual harassment, CEO exits, and anything else that may come up in a search.

"Each man has his own vocation; his talent in
his call. There is one direction in which all
space is open to him."

-*Ralph Waldo Emerson*

Appendix II: Resources for Your Job Search

If you are having trouble making it to the interview stage, you definitely need to review your job search strategy. There are many career coaches and resume gurus who will revise your resume, help you figure out what type of job you want and then wish you well on your job search; but without a search strategy, the other pieces really don't matter.

At Direction for Your Search, we can (and do) revise your resume when necessary and even coach you through career exploration, but most of the time, we don't need to. After interviewing many job seekers over the years, I have found that what most people want, and really need, is assistance with the actual job search strategy.

As a thank you for purchasing this book, I have included numerous tips and resources that will help you if you're willing to do the work necessary to get the job you want.

This list of resources has been compiled from job seekers, through my own research and many I stumbled upon by accident. I have not reviewed every website and the Internet is fluid. Should you find a resource that is objectionable or no longer providing the information described here, please accept my apology. As with any resource, it is up to you to wade through the information and determine if what is being offered is applicable and helpful to your individual situation.

General Career Advice/Information

www.careeronestop.org
Sponsored by the U.S. Department of Labor, this website provides national, state, and local career, labor market and workforce information using online tools and videos.

www.cacareerzone.org
A career exploration and planning system designed especially for students. However, job seekers can benefit from the wealth of information provided.

www.bls.gov/ooh/home.htm
The Department of Labor profiles hundreds of occupations in its Occupational Outlook Handbook. Also includes employment projects for the next decade.

www.quintcareers.com
Provides career assessment tools and tests for students, job seekers and career changers.

www.rileyguide.com
This website provides links to help you conduct a job search, explore career options, find networking and support groups, self-assessments, etc.

Job Board Aggregator

If you have ever applied for a job on a site, only to visit two or three different websites, and think to yourself, "This job looks exactly like the one I already applied for," that's because, odds are, it is the exact same job.

These websites search hundreds of job boards and company websites then compile the jobs in one place. You should review these websites to see which one you like the most; but, more than likely, you only need to visit one or two of them as they all repost the same jobs.

www.indeed.com

www.simplyhired.com

www.ziprecruiter.com

www.justjobs.com

www.jobsearchshortcuts.com

General Purpose Job Boards

If you're looking for a job, you should be well aware of the following major job search websites:

www.monster.com

www.careerbuilder.com

www.craigslist.org

www.linkedin.com

Page | 105

www.theladders.com

Specialized Job Boards

These websites specialize in I.T., healthcare, federal
government, marketing, part-time jobs, jobs for ex-offenders,
etc.

www.aapd.com
Job assistance for the disabled

www.careeronestop.org
U.S. Department of Labor Employment Centers—provides
resources for all job seekers, but can find resources for ex-
offenders, former addicts and the disabled.

www.computerjobs.com
Technology related jobs

www.dice.com
I.T. jobs

www.goodwill.org
Workforce Development Program assists people with a felony
conviction

www.gotajob.com
Student jobs/ part-time jobs

www.hard2hire.org
Jobs for ex-offenders and people with disabilities

www.healthjobsusa.com
Healthcare and medical jobs

www.nursingjobs.org
Jobs for nurses

www.talentzoo.com
Creative and marketing jobs

www.topbuildingjobs.com
Construction and homebuilding jobs

www.usajobs.opm.gov
Government jobs

Non-Profit Job Boards

www.idealist.org

www.nonprofitjobscoop.org

www.nonprofitjobs.org

www.opportunityknocks.org

Industry Associations/Professional Organizations

Most have a job board, but if not, they should have an events page where you can network with members.

ACCOUNTING/FINANCE

Accounting and Financial Women's Alliance
www.afwa.org

American Institute of Certified Public Accountants
www.aicpa.org

American Institute of Professional Bookkeepers
www.aipb.org

American Woman's Society of Certified Public Accountants
www.awscpa.org

Association of Chartered Certified Accountants
www.accaglobal.com

Association of Credit and Collection Professionals
www.acainternational.org

Chartered Institute of Management Accountants
www.cimaglobal.com

International Federation of Accountants
www.ifac.org

Institute of Management Accountants
www.imanet.org

National Association of Black Accountants
www.nabainc.org

National Association of Insurance and Financial Advisors
www.naifa.org

National Association of Tax Professionals
www.natptax.com

ADVERTISING/MARKETING

Advertising Specialty Institute
www.asicentral.com

American Academy of Advertising
www.aaasite.org

American Marketing Association
www.marketingpower.com

Association of National Advertisers
www.ana.net

Promotional Products Association International
www.ppai.org

ARCHITECURE / CONSTRUCTION

American Institute of Architects
www.aia.org

American Institute of Building Design
www.aibd.org

Association of Licensed Architects
www.alatoday.org

Association for Women in Architecture and Design
http://awa-la.org

Construction Management Association of America
http://cmaanet.org

National Association of Home Builders
www.nahb.org

National Association of Women in Construction
www.nawic.org

THE ARTS

Dance Educators of America
http://usadance.dancedea.com

Editorial Freelancers Association
www.the-efa.org

Graphic Artists Guild
www.graphicartistsguild.org

International Interior Design Association
www.iida.org

National Association of Independent Artists
www.naia-artists.org

National Cartoonists Society
www.reuben.org

National Dance Association
www.aahperd.org

National Writers Union
www.nwu.org

Organization of Black Designers
www.obd.org

Professional Association for Design
www.aiga.org

Professional Photographers of America
www.ppa.com

Society of Illustrators
www.societyillustrators.org

ENGINEERING

American Society of Civil Engineers
www.asce.org

Institute of Industrial Engineers
www.iienet.org

International Society of Certified Electronics Technicians
www.iscet.org

National Society of Black Engineers
www.nsbe.org

National Society of Professional Engineers
www.nspe.org

National Society of Women Engineers
www.swe.org

Society of Hispanic Professional Engineers
www.aotmp.com

ENTERTAINMENT/TELEVISION

American Federation of Television and Radio Artists
www.sag-aftra.org

Media Communications Association International
www.mca-i.org

National Association of Black Journalists
www.nabj.org

National Association of Broadcasters
www.nab.org

National Association for Multi-Ethnicity in Communications
www.namic.com

Journalists for Diversity
www.unityjournalists.org

HEALTHCARE

American Academy of Physician Assistants
www.aapa.org

American Association of Critical-Care Nurses
www.aacn.org

American Association of Nurse Practitioners
www.aanp.org

American Dental Hygienists Association
www.adha.org

American Health Care Association
www.ahcancal.org

American Medical Association
www.ama-assn.org

American Medical Women's Association
www.amwa-doc.org

American Nurses Association
www.nursingworld.org

American Occupational Therapy Association
www.aota.org

American Pharmacists Association
www.pharmacist.com

Association of Black Women Physicians
www.blackwomenphysicians.org

Health Industry Representatives Association
www.hira.org

International Chiropractors Association
www.chiropractic.org

National Association of Pharmaceutical Representatives
www.napsronline.org

National Federation of Licensed Practical Nurses
www.nflpn.org

National Medical Association
www.nmanet.org

Radiological Society of North America
www.rsna.org

HOSPITALITY

American Hotel and Lodging Association
www.ahla.com

Council of Hotel and Restaurant Trainers
www.chart.org

National Association for Catering and Events
www.nace.net

National Restaurant Association
www.restaurant.org

Hospitality Sales and Marketing Association International
www.hsmai.org

HUMAN RESOURCES

American Society for Training and Development
www.astd.org

American Staffing Association
www.americanstaffing.net

Association of Executive Search Consultants
www.aesc.org

Employee Assistance Professionals Association
www.eapassn.org

International Society of Certified Employee Benefit Specialists
www.iscebs.org

National Human Resources Association
www.humanresources.org

Society for Human Resource Management
www.shrm.org

Worldwide Employee Relocation Council
www.worldwideerc.org

LEGAL

American Arbitration Association
www.adr.org

American Bar Association
www.americanbar.org

The Association of Legal Assistants/ Paralegals
www.nala.org

National Association of Women Lawyers
www.nawl.org

National Bar Association
www.nationalbar.org

National Court Reports Association
www.ncra.org

National Federation of Paralegal Associations
www.paralegals.org

REAL ESTATE

Building Owners and Managers Association International
www.boma.org

Commercial Real Estate Women Network
www.crewnetwork.org

International Council of Shopping Centers
www.icsc.org

National Association of Realtors
www.realtor.org

National Association of Real Estate Brokers
www.nareb.com

Urban Land Institute
www.uli.org

RETAIL

Loss Prevention Research Council
www.lpresearch.com

National Retail Federation
www.nrf.com

Retail Industry Leaders Association
www.rila.org

TECHNOLOGY

Association for Information Systems
www.aisnet.org

Association of Information Technology Professionals
www.aitp.org

Black Data Processing Associates
www.bdpa.org

Cloud Computing Association
www.cloudcomputingassn.org

IEEE Communications Society
www.comsoc.org

Rails Girls
www.railsgirls.com

Ruby Central
www.rubycentral.org

Society for Information Management
www.simnet.org

Software & Information Industry Association
www.siia.net

Tech America
www.techamerica.org

Nationwide Temporary Agencies

One way to keep your skills sharp while unemployed is to seek temporary employment.

www.roberthalf.com

www.appleone.com

www.adeccousa.com

www.ajilon.com

Non-Profit Organizations to Volunteer Time and Expertise

Another way to keep your skills sharp while unemployed is to volunteer your time. There are lots of non-profit organizations that could benefit from your expertise and will gladly accept whatever time you can give. Volunteering with an organization can also help you gain skills when you're changing industries or if you're low on work experience.

In addition to the list of Professional Organizations and Industry Associations above, you can volunteer your time with the local chapter of one of the following organizations, which may align with you personally or professionally:

American Alliance of Museums
www.aam-us.org

American Heart Association
www.heart.org

American Personal & Private Chef Association
www.personalchef.com

American Red Cross
www.redcross.org

Association of Image Consultants International
www.aici.org

Boys & Girls Clubs of America
www.bgca.org

Chamber of Commerce – Almost every city has at least one

Dress for Success
www.dressforsuccess.org

Girl Scouts of America
www.girlscouts.org

Girls Inc.
www.girlsinc.org

Girl Start
www.girlstart.org

Humane Society of the United States
www.humanesociety.org

Institute of Management Consultants
www.imcusa.org

International Association of Administrative Professionals
www.iaap-hq.org

MBA Women International
www.mbawomen.org

National Alliance on Mental Illness
www.nami.org

National Association of Women Business Owners
www.nawbo.org

National Black MBA Association
www.nbmbaa.org

National Society for Hispanic MBAs
www.nshmba.org

Step Up Women's Network
www.suwn.org

United Friends of the Children
www.unitedfriends.org

United Way of America
www.unitedway.org

University Alumni Associations – your school has one

Obviously this list is not exhaustive, but is filled with large well-known non-profits and smaller organizations with which I encourage you to spend some time.

Employment Discrimination Assistance

www.dol.gov/dol/topic/discrimination
The Department of Labor has two agencies which deal with EEO (Equal Employment Opportunity) monitoring and enforcement, the Civil Rights Center and the Office of Federal Contract Compliance Programs. The link provides information about both.

www.eeoc.gov/employees/howtofile.cfm
The Equal Employment Opportunity Commission (EEOC) is an independent federal agency that promotes equal opportunity in employment through administrative and judicial enforcement of the federal civil rights laws. This link provides assistance in filing a claim.

www.las-elc.org
The Legal Aid Society–Employment Law Center is a nonprofit, legal services organization assisting California's low-income working families for more than 90 years. The Legal Aid Society of New York is the oldest organization providing assistance since 1876. Check with your city for information on your local organization.

www.bettzedek.org
Founded in 1974, Bet Tzedek is a 501(c)3 non-profit
organization that provides free legal representation to low-
income residents of Los Angeles County. They assist with
cases related to workers' rights such as retaliation, wage and
hour and worker safety, in addition to consumer rights, elder
law and housing issues. If you don't reside in Los Angeles
County, CA, you can find similar assistance by conducting an
Internet search.

www.legalmomentum.org
Legal Momentum is the nation's oldest legal defense and
education fund dedicated to advancing the rights of all women
and girls. For more than 40 years they have advocated for
public policy changes, including increasing pathways into
quality employment opportunities and protecting workplace
rights of vulnerable populations.

www.hirenetwork.org
Established by the Legal Action Center in 2001, the National
Helping Individuals with criminal records Re-enter through
Employment (H.I.R.E.) Network is both a national
clearinghouse for information and an advocate for policy
change. The goal of the National H.I.R.E. Network is to
increase the number and quality of job opportunities available
to people with criminal records by changing public policies,
employment practices and public opinion.

About the Author

Stacey A. Gordon, MBA is a dynamic job coach and charismatic speaker, on the topics of networking and career success. She also runs a successful boutique recruiting company with a focus on diversity. She has a passion for connecting people and creating synergies which make her career workshops and networking presentations interactive and fun-filled, with an immediate impact on the participants. Though she enjoys showing job seekers how to find a job they will love, kick their careers into high-gear, or increase their job prospects via effective networking, Stacey especially likes catering to college students, Baby Boomers and the long-term unemployed because each group has their own unique set of challenges. She has been quoted in *Essence Magazine*, is a contributing writer for *ForbesWoman* and has appeared on FoxBusiness.com.

Born in the UK, Stacey has an interesting perspective on race, culture, and careers. A wife, and mom to three daughters, she graduated *Cum Laude* from St. John's University in New York and earned an MBA in Entrepreneurial Management at Pepperdine University's Graziado School of Business & Management.

Stacey can be found at www.DirectionForYourSearch.com, while The Gordon Group resides on the web at www.TheGordonGroup.biz.

Jump Start Your Job Search

Unlike a career coach, a job coach guides you through the process of getting a job, changing industries or starting over.

Obtaining a job is very hard work . . . it can take as much time as a full time job.

With Direction for Your Search coaching strategies, much of the work is completed for you. If you are currently employed and seeking a new job, it is difficult to find the time to work on your resume, conduct proper research and put a cohesive strategy in place. If you're unemployed or just getting started in your career, a strategy is no less necessary. In fact, it is decidedly more important, since you are, unfortunately, a less desirable candidate.

Stacey takes some of the apprehension out of the interview process and job search process as a whole. Can your job search benefit from any of the following:

- Formulating answers to some of the difficult interview questions
- Coaching around challenging gaps in your employment history
- Tools to use to build a network to aid your specific job search
- Making you, as a candidate, stand out from the other job applicants
- Assessment of your skills and experience
- Resume review

If you would like individual attention, or assistance with implementing a job search strategy, schedule a private consultation at www.directionforyoursearch.com to address your needs.

NOTES

Made in the USA
San Bernardino, CA
17 March 2013